Spirit Driven Messages For Everyday Life

Cara Elise Kennon

ISBN: 1495216888
ISBN 13: 9781495216886

Dedication

I dedicate this book to my first love, my best friend, and my constant companion, Jesus Christ. Without your love and acceptance, I would have never had the strength to change my life. From the day I accepted salvation, you have walked with me every step of the way. You never turned from me, even when I walked in the wrong direction. I am transformed. Once I was a caterpillar, and now I am a butterfly. Thank you for the beautiful wings you have given me to fly.

Acknowledgments

O ne day while I was in a counseling session with Carl, my Christian counselor, he said, "Cara, you need to write a book." I looked at him with my eyes popped and my mouth wide open, and I said, "Are you kidding me?" I explained that I barely finished the ninth grade. I make up my own words at times, and he thought I should write a book? He told me, "Just sit down and start with 'I was born on…' and let God do the rest." That was more than ten years ago. I did exactly as he said: I sat down and wrote, I was born on…"

I continued to write about my life, but it took a turn and I started writing messages. As the years went on and my relationship with Christ grew stronger and stronger, the messages became so much better, because they were spirit driven. Carl was one of the most incredible people I ever had the privilege to meet, let alone counsel with. He helped me get back on the path to living a Christ-centered life. He saw something in me I could not see in myself. I am forever grateful for his presence in my life.

I met Carl because my Stephen Minister-turned-best-friend told me about him. Bonnie and I come from two totally different backgrounds, yet we are so connected. I am who I am today because of her presence, her counsel, her friendship, and her love. She has been a mother, a big sister, and a friend. She opened her whole family to my daughter and me, and I love each and every one of the Strickers.

Everyone needs close friends, and I have been blessed to have abundant friends that have been around forever. Paula, you were the first friend I had that truly loved and accepted me. You have been my spiritual mentor, my sister, my "person," and I love you so much. I will never forget sitting in the car with you several years ago, crying because I didn't want to go into the local business to introduce myself and give them my messages to display. You sat there and encouraged me till I got out of the car. You have been beside me every step of the way, and I am forever grateful for that. Aletha, I am a believer and follower of Christ because of the seeds you and your family planted so many years ago. You are one of my best friends, and I would not want to do life without you.

To my family, Aunt Judy and Uncle Herb, Aunt Shelly and Uncle Bob, Uncle Alan and Rose, and Josh and Frankie: thank you for accepting me and my beliefs. You have all supported me over the years, and I love each of you so very much.

To my parents, who are no longer here: your choices in life had many consequences that affected your children. I thank you for that. The negative impact of those choices gave me a testimony that God can turn anything to gold. Romans 8:28 is real: "In all things God works for the good for those who love him, who have been called according to his purpose." I harbor no bitterness and am just grateful to God that we were able to heal and mend. I loved you each so very dearly. I miss you both every day.

I saved the best for last...my daughter, Erica. You will never know what you have brought to my life, the joy and the happiness. I have learned and grown so much by being your mother. Whenever the road got tough and I felt bad about myself, God told me to see the reflection in you—to look to you and I would see who I was. You are goodness, filled with such light and love. I love you from the depth of my being and with all my heart. xoxo

Foreword

S pirit-driven messages. That is what I call every message I write. Most of the time when I sit down to write a message, I have nothing to say. I ask the Lord, "Lord, what should I write about this month?" Before I know it, I have a "spirit-driven message."

I have been writing spirit-driven messages since 2009. This book is a collection of some of my favorite messages. Several are written during holiday season and reference that time of year.

In July 2012 I wrote a message called "Why Do I Believe?" I have included it here as my forward. It gives you some insight to who I am, why I believe, and why I write these messages.

WHY DO I BELIEVE?

I spoke with a person the other day who told me that he believed in God but that Jesus was a prophet and that he did not believe in the trinity. He said that he and I should not really talk about religion, because we didn't see eye to eye. Since I consider myself not so much a religious person but more of a spiritual person, I wanted to let him know why I believed what I did. What is was for me.

It had nothing to do with religion but everything to do with a relationship. I thought that I would share my story, my testimony with my readers. You have gotten bits and pieces, but I really want you all to know why I love Jesus, why I believe. This is a short-story version, but I am writing a book all about my life and hope to get it published one day. It really is the story of God, how amazing he is, and why I am devoted to him forever.

My family is Jewish, for those of you that do not know that. I was raised in foster care run by the Jewish Federation. My mom abandoned my brother and me when I was about three, and for a year or more I lived with my grandmother and in a shelter in the Bronx waiting to be placed with a family. My dad felt he could not take care of two little kids, so I guess you can say he abandoned us too, even though he would come and visit.

The shelter was not a nice place. Set up orphanage-style, we slept on cots; I was on the lower level, and my brother, Josh, since he was older, was on the upper level. We were not placed together when the time came for us to leave.

Once placed with a family, I attended Hebrew school and celebrated all the Jewish holidays. No bread during Passover, fasting on Yom Kipper—in all aspects I was a practicing Jew. Only one thing was missing: I did not believe in God. I did not believe there was a God. I had no interest in anything related to God, and I just went through the motions. If there was a God, where was he? Why was I in a foster home? Why was my brother in a different kind of home far from me, and I hardly got to see him? And most importantly, where were my parents, and why didn't they want us? I am sure you can imagine how at a very young age I felt unlovable, unwanted, and rejected.

After all, if your parents don't want you, if you feel your parents don't love you, who would?

I left foster care at the age of twelve to go live with my mother in California. The things I would witness and be involved in are things no young girl should see or do. After eight months my mom sent me to live with my dad and brother, because she ran out of money and couldn't afford me anymore (or that is what she told me anyway).

Living with my dad was awful. He was mean and did not know how to handle two teenage age kids. Now, anyone who has or has had teenagers knows how hard those years can be. Well, take two kids who grew up as my brother and I did—very disciplined lives—and then put us with parents we never really lived with and who had no real rules. What do you think you would get? Sure, my brother and I went to the Jewish sleepaway camp (overnight for the whole summer), and we belonged to Jewish clubs for kids (kind of like youth programs in Christian churches). But you could not convince me there was a God.

My father used to tell me he was God. He would tell me, "If the sun is shining but I tell you it is raining, you better go get an umbrella." My father would tell me I was a zero, a nothing, and I would never be anything more than a babysitter. If I did something wrong, he would say, "I should have left you in the home," or threaten to send me back. So when someone like that tells you he is God, I am sure you can understand how there was no way I would be convinced of any kind of God.

By the time I was nineteen, I was broken in a million pieces. My mom and I had one more "encounter," I will say, when I was fifteen, and it ended with her making perfectly clear I was not a priority and I was not wanted. I was crushed. In my book I explain it as "that is when my soul cracked." I felt like a nothing, a nobody. I felt abandoned, unwanted, and rejected even more than in my younger years.

In a turn of events, at the age of twenty...Jesus reached down, and I grabbed on for dear life. I felt him all over me and in me once I accepted him as my savior. I needed a savior so bad. For the first time I felt accepted even in all my flaws, in all my sin. I felt loved. That love and acceptance gave me strength to change my life, to rebuild, to renew my mind: "I can do all things in Christ who strengthens me" (Philippians 4:13).

Now, I did sort of think I was going to be this bright new shiny penny the day after I was saved, but that surely did NOT happen. It has been a long journey. I had so much work to do. I had to reprogram my mind from all the wrong messages I received as a child. I had to surrender all. I had to forgive and release the pain and the anger that I had toward my parents. There were times I strayed from God and made unwise choices, and although I was always forgiven and received grace and mercy from my heavenly father, there were consequences to walk through. I had to parent my daughter with no role model at all and all the while parent myself too!

But God is so amazing. His grace and mercy are real. His love is unconditional. He never leaves you. He never fails you. He took all those years of "bad" and made the light shine. Look where I am today. Look what I am doing, what story I am telling. Before my parents both passed away, I had nothing but love for each of them. I was totally at peace, and I was a good daughter. I respected them and made sure they both knew how much I loved them. There was no bitterness, no anger, no hurt feelings. My daughter is amazing…not just because of all the love and acceptance I gave to her but because I prayed all the time for the Holy Spirit to help me parent this child.

In the last four years, I lost both my parents somewhat suddenly, my mother within six months of being diagnosed and my father within seven weeks. I myself lost my home, my daughter left for college, and then I got cancer. Through all this, God was faithful. He walked with me each and every day. On the days I could not walk—he carried me. On the days I was overwhelmed, he breathed new life in me to keep going. When I needed a word, when I needed to make decisions, I cried out and asked him what to do, and he spoke to me, in a way and with a word that I KNEW it was him talking directly to me. During the death of my parents, I felt the peace that surpasses all understanding, and as I look back I completely see all the good and none of the bad.

This is why I believe what I do. I believe there is one true God, one son who died on a cross for me, for my sin, so that I may have eternal life. Who left a helper, the Holy Spirit with me—to guide me. Jesus is the bridge that gets me to my heavenly father. I don't have all the answers to the questions. I don't know why bad things happen. I don't know why some Bible stories seem so unreal. But here's the thing: I don't need to know. I don't need anyone to break it down for me and try to get me to see it their way. I have all the proof I need. I have forty-eight years to look back on and see for myself what a mighty God I serve. When I didn't know him, he surely knew me. He knows my name, he knows every hair on my head (Luke 12:7), and he knit me just so in my mother's womb (Psalm 139:13). I know this not because the Bible tells me so but because I feel it every single day. I see it all around me.

These newsletters that I write are from my soul and are guided by the Holy Spirit. Not to glorify me, but to glorify Him. To encourage you and give you hope. I am an open book. I am the clay and he is the potter. I am so passionate about what I believe and sharing the good news. We were meant to live victoriously. To live joyfully and abundantly.

Table of Contents

Why Do Bad Things Happen?

I so wish I had an answer to that. I wish I could just tell you why the good die young, why children suffer, why we go through circumstances that cause us so much pain, and why there are crimes of such horror. I don't have an answer. I can only share my viewpoint and some of my story.

First, bad things are going to happen. It is inevitable. No one gets away from circumstances that shake you, and no one ever cheats death. Sometimes circumstances happen that are bad and you had nothing to do with it.

When I was a little girl, my mother put my brother and me on a bus, gave us name tags, and took off. She abandoned her children. My father felt he could not care for a three- and five-year-old, so we went to a shelter and awaited placement into foster care. My family is Jewish, so we were in homes run by the Jewish Federation. We were split up, and I lived in foster care till I was twelve. I did not believe there was a God. I went to Hebrew school and all that, but I tuned everything out. I thought to myself, "If there was a God, then why am I living in a foster home? Did I do something bad? Did I deserve this?"

Then, when I went to live with my dad as a teenager, he used to tell me he was God. You can only imagine what kind of attitude I had when someone tried to talk to me about God and Jesus, right?

I was saved at twenty. I felt the hand of Jesus reaching down to grip mine. The journey I have traveled has been tough. Sometimes things were so bad I didn't know if I could get to the next step, and sometimes things were so amazingly great I just sat and cried tears of joy for an hour.

At forty-eight what I have come to know without a doubt is that everything that has happened, bad or good, was to get me to this time in life and every moment to come. I enjoy and savor life's moments. I use all that was bestowed upon me to help others, to encourage others, and I LOVE to tell my story to anyone that wants to hear it. Not because of me but because of what God has done in me.

I counsel people, in case you did not know that. I am a HOPE mentor. I am the person my friends call to get encouragement. Those are the gifts I get to enjoy because of bad things that happened to me in life. Those are the blessings I have received.

I heard in our sermon yesterday, "What are you going to do with what God has given you?" That to me means all circumstances, good or bad. As I drove to work this morning, I was thinking about the luncheon I was going to speak at today. It was for the American Cancer Society. I started crying as I drove to work, because "What are you going to do with what God has given you?" came to mind and I thought, "I had cancer and I survived, and now I am going to speak about that, my treatments, my recovery, and how I really feel blessed to be in a position to do so." Cancer was a bad thing that happened to me, but even while I was going through my treatments I could see the good God was doing. Not just to me but to those around me.

I always say it is about perspective, about attitude. We will *all* have circumstances that we do not want to be in, that we do not understand, and that we feel we do not deserve. It is ok to talk to God about it. It's ok to get angry, hurt, and upset. Tell him how you feel, tell him you do not understand. Allow him to change you in your circumstance, and, more importantly, allow him to give you peace. I can testify that there really is a peace that surpasses all understanding. It is a calm like nothing you have ever experienced before. It's like your whole world is spinning around you, yet you are as still as you can be.

I am sorry that you have had circumstances that are bad. I have heard so many stories over the years—diseases, molestation, addictions, relationship issues, and death. I don't have an answer for why that happened to you or someone you know. But I know, with every breath in my body, that you *can* trust God, that he *will* bring you through it, and that you will see blessings over time.

My favorite Bible verse is Isaiah 49:15–16: "I will not forget you. See, I have inscribed you on the palms of my hands."

Are You Hopeless?

I looked up the word *hopeless* to see what words were used to define it. This is what I found: despairing, bleak, no possibility of solution, a loss of confidence.

Do you feel hopeless? Is life throwing you boulders, and each one knocks you down just a bit more? Have you been looking for a job for months with no prospects in site? Is there illness with a loved one, and you cannot see recovery in the future? Have your children gone astray, and no matter what you do you can't seem to get them back on track? Have you been praying and crying out to the Lord and still feel abandoned and forsaken? Hopeless. No possibility of a solution and a loss of confidence.

There is hope, though. There is a possibility of a solution, and we can have confidence. Trials and tribulations are going to come. That is one thing you can count on for sure in life. You will have trials and tribulations. Just like we are going to die one day. No one escapes it. Not even Jesus. Jesus had so many trials and tribulations, don't you agree? In the garden of Gethsemane, Jesus prayed, "'Father, if you are willing, take this cup from me; yet not my will, but your will be done.' An Angel from heaven appeared to him and strengthened him. And being in *anguish*, he prayed more earnestly, and his sweat was like drops of blood falling to the ground" (Luke 22:42–44).

Sounds like Jesus was hopeless, right? Despair, bleak, no possibility of solution. I don't think Jesus lost his confidence, but he was for sure afraid. He did not want "his cup." The key here is, even though Jesus did not want the dread of the trials ahead, he *reaffirmed his commitment to what God wanted.*

That's the difference between us and Jesus. He reaffirmed, while we try to run away. He looks up; we look every which way but up. We not only lose hope but lose faith, and then we start to question, "Is there really a God?"

The most important part of our relationship with God is trust. If we trust him, we will weather anything that comes our way. See, when things are going good, we forget. We don't arm ourselves with those Bible verses we did when we were hopeless and suffering. We don't dive into his word every day like we did when we were holding on for dear life. It has to be an everyday thing with God. You have to be so planted in the word, in his presence, in his love, that when that storm comes—and you can be assured it will—you will stand firmly planted.

Did you know that when Jesus went to the cross he was separated from God? He had to be separated from God in order to die for the world's sin. This is something we as believers will *NEVER* have to worry about.

"For I am convinced that neither death nor life, neither angels nor demons, neither the present nor the future, nor any powers, neither height nor depth, nor anything else in all creation, will be able to separate us from the love of God that is in Christ Jesus our Lord" (Romans 8:38–39).

This was the first Bible verse I learned as a new believer. That no matter what my circumstance is, no matter how hopeless it may *look*, I need not be hopeless. I can be hopeful! I can have faith that it will all work out and that God, who loves me so much, will never leave me, never forsake me.

I know for some of you things seem and look so hopeless. I know you have prayed and you cry out and you just really feel that God has left you. You have to believe. You have to choose to still put your faith in what you cannot see. You have to remember that "the will of God will never take you where the grace of God cannot protect you." You have to *choose* to trust him through the circumstance and rest in his peace that he promised to every believer.

I pray that this holiday season is filled with an abundance of peace and love and joy. I pray that we all remember that it is not about material gifts but about gifting someone encouragement, uplifting someone, reaching out to those less fortunate. I also pray the New Year is bright for each of you, and I thank you for allowing me to share my journey with you.

Religion v. Relationship

Today our pastor made reference to "religion v. relationship," and it stuck with me all day. I thought back to when I was an unbeliever of God and Jesus and how I viewed religion at that time. Because I was raised under the Jewish faith, in my younger years I really didn't think anything. I enjoyed the holidays, didn't really pay attention in Hebrew school, and "religion v. relationship" never even dawned on me.

As a teenager so very far away from God, temple, church, or anything even remotely close, I know I surely did not like people telling me "you need Jesus" or "you need to go to church." As I looked around me and looked at "church goers" I knew, friends' parents who went to church, I did not see a place I would want to belong to. I had a friend whose parents were so big in their church, praised by the church for all they "did," and yet outside of church they were abusing their children. They were not in any way people I would follow to a church.

When I was about nineteen—shortly before I surrendered my life to Christ—I was working for a woman that was a believer. I was doing a lot of cocaine during those days. I taught aerobics for a living, and before each shift I would snort about a quarter gram. That, along with hours of teaching exercise, made me extremely hyper. The pulse would beat out the side of my neck and I would get anxious, and my boss would tell me it was just "the devil" trying to mess with me. Now, I can tell you that "You need Jesus" and "The devil is trying to mess with you" were NOT what was going to make me come to the Lord. In fact, I wanted to be even further away than I was. She, another believer, and I had to go away for a weekend aerobic instruction class, and for the whole three-hour drive these ladies were telling me how I needed to turn to Jesus and away from my party ways. They spoke of religion and never shared with me "the relationship"—their testimony. I could not wait to get away from them. Nothing they said to me was inviting.

Last month I told you about my friend's mom who planted the seed. She did that by her actions, by the way she was around me. She never once said, "Cara, you need Jesus," or anything like that. I now think it was because she was in a relationship rather than a religion mindset, and my boss and coworker were more in a religion mindset than a relationship. Does this make sense? Are you still with me?

It's kind of like this: Why do you try to live a life of obedience to God? Do you do it out of fear of what he will do or out of love for who he is? I think in religion we try to be obedient out of fear, and in a relationship we try out of love. For my spirituality, I do it out of love. I am so in love with Jesus. I love God SOOOOOOO much I don't want to inhibit my love for him with disobedience. Do I sin? YES. And I fall short. And when I do, I am so remorseful. I am so remorseful because I so love him. HE and I are in a relationship.

I am glad I did not grow up in church. There was nothing to pollute my mind. When I became a believer, I found this small, wooden Presbyterian church in Connecticut, and it was all love, all fellowship, and the pastor was so inviting. When I came to Georgia, I went to a few churches and got yelled at by the pastor—fire and brimstone, rules and regulations. All I thought to myself was, "How would anyone, *why* would anyone want to try to build a relationship like that?"

I don't like it when people call me "religious." I am so far from that. I consider myself more spiritual. I have the Holy Spirit that guides me, and I have a loving relationship with someone I cannot see. But I feel Jesus. His love and acceptance transformed me. It healed me. "He heals the brokenhearted and binds up their wounds" (Psalm 147:3).

I can totally testify that that promise is true. He healed my broken heart and my shattered soul, and he bound up my wounds. That's a relationship. No "religion" on Earth can do what he did. "For God so loved the world that he gave his one and only Son, that whoever believes in him shall not perish but have eternal life" (John 3:16). I know I certainly want to be in a relationship with that being.

I encourage any believer: share what God has done for you. Let the light of the Lord shine from within you. People who see by actions and transformation will want to know who is behind that.

"This little light of mine...I'm gonna let it shine...let it shine, let it shine, let it shine."

Mountaintops and Valleys

66 "The Lord our God spoke to us in Horeb, saying: 'You have dwelt long enough at this mountain'" (Deuteronomy 1:6).

That was my word today. I was going to do a message called "What Is Your Perspective?" and when I saw this verse I realized mountaintops and valleys are about perspective.

Wouldn't it be great to always be at the mountaintop? I love when I am at the top. Life is just fabulous, the storm has come and gone, and I have reached new heights. I just want to stay there forever. What I have noticed, though, is what makes it so great up there at the top is the climb to get there, the valley I started in. What I have also come to know is that when I'm in the valley is when I am at weakest point and have no other choice but to ask God for help. I am at my lowest place, and I can do nothing in my own strength.

I try, though. I think that I am bigger than my problems, and I try feverishly to figure it all out.

At this stage in life, that doesn't last long. I remember that I am not in control and that if I have done all I can do, I have no other option than to trust God.

Trusting God is to see his blessing during the hike up. I totally believe each of us has some situation they can look back on and see the handiwork of God.

I know a young man who is so trying to do everything right. He has turned his life around. One and a half years ago, he had three garbage bags to his name, was sleeping on the floor in a friend's house, and had no job and not even enough money for a haircut. He enrolled in college at the age of twenty-one. It was a tough year and a half, but he made it through. He has a job, just got all A's this summer, and has an apartment. And all I can see is the handiwork of God. Nothing comes easy for him. At every turn the enemy jumps right in. He gets weary and discouraged, and I keep telling him to trust God, to look back and see that although it feels like the valley, he is really on the mountaintop.

In my devotional for today, in which I saw the verse above, I saw my journal notes from 2009. (I like to read old devotions—you always learn something new!) I want to share, because we forget so easily when we are not at the top of the mountain. I wrote, "Please help me to always remember that if I am in the battle (valley), my mountaintop is around the corner, and if I am on the mountaintop you are *preparing* me for the next battle (valley)."

So what perspective will you look at things with? Trusting God for all things means exactly that. Yes, our human flesh will rise up, and anxiety, fear, and worry will *try* to cover us. But the Bible tells us these things have no hold on us: "Fear not, I am with you" (Isaiah 41:10); "Do not be anxious for anything" (Philippians 4:6); and "Do not worry about tomorrow" (Matthew 6:34).

One last thing to think about. Ask yourself this question and answer it honestly: If your life was all mountaintops, would you ever lean on God, feel the need for God? If you never had trials and tribulations, would you think you did everything in your own strength?

In the valleys is where we are forced to cry out to Jesus. It's when we are at our weakest that we can truly surrender all.

Make a choice to look through the God lens. Have hope in the midst of the battle and growth of the valley, then, when you get to the top of that mountain, the view will be like nothing you have ever experienced.

Just Live

I was sitting at my desk and this thought came to my mind: *Just Live.* Simple, easy, and carefree.

I only have to live. I don't need to worry, don't need to plan beyond the immediate; all I need to do is Just Live.

I had this sense that I can live confidently that God has me in the palm of his hand (Isaiah 49:15–16) and I need do nothing but Just Live.

I was reading some blogs about the side effects of some medicine I have to take to help prevent a reoccurrence of cancer. A year ago when I read all those blogs, they frightened me. Now I realize all I have to do is live. I will tackle any side effects with God right by my side. I certainly don't need to worry or be fearful. After all, what could I possibly do anyway?

Ever feel like that? Ever think, "Gee, I worried about this situation and, truth be told, there was nothing I could have done anyway. It was a waste of time and energy, and what I was worried about never even came to pass."

Confidence in who HE is. Confidence in HIS ability. Confidence in HIS strength.

I heard a sermon once, and the pastor said, "Being a Christian is having confidence that God is who he said he is and that he will do everything he promised."

What would that look like for you? What if you awoke every day leaving all your cares and burdens to God? Could you? Do you want to try?

In order to do that, one would have to live by faith—totally. In order to Just Live, you would have to release it all, surrender all your cares and all your worries and be at peace.

Just Live!

You know, I was sitting at the pool the other day discussing with my friend the "peace that transcends all understanding" (Philippians 4:7). When you have this peace, when it comes upon you, you can Just Live every day, no matter what comes your way. What the Bible means by "transcends all understanding" is that many of those around you will not understand; they will not understand why you are not frazzled, or worried, or anxious. The peace, the Just Live attitude will not be understood by many, but I can assure you it will leave a lasting impression on most.

A great Bible verse I love is John 14:27: "Peace I leave with you; my peace I give you. I do not give to you as the world gives. Do not let your hearts be troubled and do not be afraid."

Just Live!

Wake up tomorrow and decide that you're going to Just Live. Say, "I'm making a choice to give God all my cares, all my worries, and in return he is going to give me his peace."

If those cares and worries start to creep into your thoughts, shoo them away with the Bible verse above and tell yourself God said, "Peace I leave with you."

His peace he gives me. No one here on Earth can give to me as he does. I am *not* to let my heart be troubled and I need *not* be afraid. Instead all I need to do is Just Live.

Diamonds Are a Girl's Best Friend

I know: if diamonds are a girl's best friend, what about the boys? While this month's newsletter is geared more to my beautiful girls, it can certainly apply to the boys as well.

Last year's newsletter for October was called "A Little Chemo and Humor for October." It touched a lot on my journey through being vain and how God just worked that right out of me during my chemo treatment. I think that every woman should shave her head just once so she can see the real beauty she is, as God sees her. The diamond that she is. I read the quote below somewhere, and I saved it because it was so powerful:

> If you look at a diamond ring under a microscope every day and become intimately familiar with its flaws, you might be embarrassed by it. But that is not how God made the beauty of diamonds to be seen. The beauty of a diamond is seen when someone holds it up in the sunlight and everyone can see it sparkle.

Let's put this in our world, our society. We are always being looked at under a microscope, yes? Are there people in your life that look at you under a microscope all the time and point out your every flaw? A husband or mate? Your boss? Maybe your parents, children, or a friend? What about yourself or society?

Isn't it normal to point out the things you don't like about yourself so you can start "working on them"? I know when I talk to my girlfriends, sometimes we discuss the things we don't like about ourselves—our age, our hair, our weight, our clothes, our this, our that…It stinks! Doesn't society say you need to be thin and beautiful, and if you're not they pick you apart like they are peeling a shrimp? How awful. How about when you were a child or teenager and your parent always had to talk about the things you did WRONG? "You're not doing well in school," "You drive too fast," "You eat too much," "You this," "You that." Do you get my point here?

So what happens to us? Do we feel good? Do we feel joyful? Do we feel like a diamond? Like a light that is held up to shine and sparkle? I think not.

We are God's treasures, his diamonds. He crafted each one of us to sparkle and shine a beautiful light. There are no two that are alike; we are each one of a kind. Imagine if every little girl grew up thinking she was a diamond. (Really sit and marinate on that for a minute.) No one ever pointed out her flaws (notice I didn't say "mistakes"), and she was loved and made to feel like a treasure, a gem, a jewel. How many women can say they grew up like that? Not me. But here's the thing: God has loved each little girl like that ALL HER LIFE. (And boys too.) God never points out your flaws to you. He corrects things that hold you back, he allows consequences to befall you, and he warns you. But he is the one and only being that does not "pick" on you. Even if we think we are the best parents in the world, we're not. Only God is the best parent. We are not capable of being perfect parents, because we are human.

God created each of us in our own uniqueness, each one of us hand carved, so to speak. I know it's hard to believe that, but it is true. "For you formed my inward parts; you knitted me together in my mother's womb" (Psalm 139:13). For those of us that are parents, I know this to be true. If you put in the time, if you put forth the effort, you will see sparkle. Meaning if you treasure your child like a diamond—like the gem, the jewel God *entrusted* you with—your child will grow up with sparkle and shine. If you trash your gem, toss it aside, don't pay much attention to it, neglect it, and don't clean it up, the sparkle diminishes.

We are all like jewels. We were someone's diamond, and the level of care we were given determines how much we shine and sparkle. For me, I had no shine and no sparkle—none, zip, zero. But then I was saved, and I allowed Jesus Christ to come in and polish me up and clean me out. He took care of me and gave me a place to rest and be loved and nurtured, and today I shine and I sparkle. I shine his light for the entire world to see. Before my cancer and chemo, I still picked myself apart, focusing on all my flaws. I am grateful I had to sacrifice my appearance during recovery, because it allowed me to see myself as a diamond. It allowed me to stop looking at myself under a microscope daily and to just rest in the knowledge that I am "fearfully and wonderfully made."

Father Knows Best

I read a story the other day in the book of 2 Kings. It was the story of King Hezekiah. Hezekiah was the thirteenth king of Judah. He was a man who had a relationship with God and with whom God was pleased. In 2 Kings 18:5–6 we read, "Hezekiah trusted in the Lord, the God of Israel. There was no one like him among all Kings of Judah, either before him or after him. He held fast to the Lord and did not cease to follow him; he kept the commandments the Lord had given Moses." Over a hundred-year period of Judah's history, Hezekiah was the only faithful king.

Later on in Hezekiah's life, he became ill. The Lord sent a prophet to tell Hezekiah to "get his house in order, because you are going to die; you will not recover" (2 Kings 20:1). The Bible tells us that Hezekiah "wept bitterly" for the Lord to spare his life. God loved Hezekiah and in his permissive will granted him fifteen more years to live.

Now, before I continue the story, let's take a 2011 check on this, shall we? Isn't it true that when things are going great we feel we are 100 percent in God's will? We are following God's will, and we know "Father knows best." We trust the Lord for all things, and we are sailing along. Then something shifts and our circumstances change. The water is bumpy and the tide is high. We went from being at the mountaintop to finding ourselves in the valley. Do we still have the same trust in God as we did when all was good? Do we still believe that "Father knows best"? Do we respond to our heavenly father with "Whatever your will, Lord, I'm ok with"?

That has been a tough one for me to get under my skin. It's hard for me to be in the valley and think that this is part of God's plan. As a parent I spent my entire child's life trying to keep her from the valley, to keep her high on the mountaintop. As I relate that to God, and me being his child, well, I find my trust waivers.

After I read the next part of the Hezekiah story, I thought to myself, "I am so grateful for time gone by. It allows me to look back and see that God's plan has *always* been the best plan, the best route. I grow, I learn, and I become more faithful." Let's continue…

During those added fifteen years, Manasseh was born, and he eventually succeeded Hezekiah as King of Judah. Manasseh, who reigned for fifty-five years, was the most evil king ever to rule over Judah. Manasseh encouraged idolatry throughout the nation. He passed his own son through fire according to the abominable practices of idolatry. He shed much innocent blood during his reign; every part of the nation suffered from his cruelty. Manasseh's wickedness provoked God to anger, but Manasseh ignored God's warning. All these hardships were caused by Manasseh, a king *who would have never been born* if Hezekiah would have accepted God's will for his life. Lastly, Hezekiah's extended reign led to Judah's eventual defeat by the Babylonians.

I tell you, I will forever be changed in the way I pray after reading that. I thought about my prayer life and how I pray. So many times I have pleaded with God. So many times I have prayed and told him what I wanted, what I needed (or what I thought I needed). Because I am older and wiser and time has passed, I have many situations to look back on and KNOW "Father knew best."

Garth Brooks has a song, and one of the lyrics says, "I thank God for unanswered prayers." A *no* from God does not mean he has forgotten us. When I tell my daughter no, it's not because I don't love her; it's because Mommy knows best.

When life is good and you are on the mountaintop praising God for his will in our lives, make sure you take a snapshot of that and hold on to it for the times you are in the valley. No one escapes hard times. Peace that surpasses all understanding, comfort that is beyond human comprehension, and faith for the things we cannot see are exactly what we need to grasp as we accept God's will for our life and remember "Father knows best."

Smorgasbord

I could not pinpoint what to write about this month. I started and stopped a few different messages. All of a sudden, right now, on December 2, at 12:15 p.m., it all came to me. It's kind of a "smorgasbord" message, a variety of topics.

One thing I think about is how grateful I am for all my blessings, my family, my friends, and my savior. I really do not know how people with no belief in God make it through. I don't want to offend anyone; please forgive me if that statement does. I just know from my own experience, my own trials and tribulations, I would not make it through without my constant companion, Jesus.

It's been a rough couple of days. I got in a fender bender, and my daughter is having trials of her own, life lessons she is learning. And I am most grateful that all this turmoil will not steal my joy or my peace. I'm not saying that my blood pressure isn't rising, but I can easily breathe it out. I'm not in charge, I don't have to be, and I know God will take care of everything.

I also have been thinking about what truly matters in life. I was recently in a beautiful home. It was put together so exquisitely; I loved everything about this home. As I walked through this home, I thought, "Would I trade my life, what I have been through, to have this home, the cars in the driveway, the pool, the lake?" My answer was a quick no.

To share a bit, that home and lifestyle could have easily been mine: it was the home of my ex-husband. All I thought was that none of this "stuff" matters. It didn't matter then, thirteen years ago, and it doesn't matter now. My greatest gifts are my precious child and the relationship I have with my Lord and savior. My family and friends mean more to me than any price tag, and although I do love Christmas, it's not about the presents; it's about the warmth, the closeness to those I care about. It's about "What can I do to help someone? What can I give?" It doesn't have to be material things. It could be a simple gift of time, compassion, or a hug to someone who really needs one.

I strive to be more Christ-like daily. I fall down plenty, but I have this amazing heavenly father who is right there to help me get up, tell me how much I am loved, dust me off, and send me on my way. That is Christmas. That's the present God gave to all of us.

Christmas is not really a holiday celebration; it's a birthday celebration. A day to honor what God gave to us. "For God so loved the world that he gave his one and only son that whoever believes in him will not perish but have eternal life" (John 3:16). That's the best present one could have.

I pray that each of you have peace beyond measure and joy that overflows. I pray that you look past the material things and see the gifts that God has bestowed upon each of you.

Moving On Up

"**W**ere moving on up, to the east side, to a deluxe apartment in the sky. We're moving on up; we finally got a piece of the pie…"

Do you know that jingle? That is from *The Jeffersons*. I found myself singing that as I thought about graduation time. My daughter will be a senior in college next year, and she will be graduating. This summer, like last, she will be in New York City doing an internship. She is "moving on up," and by next year she will decide what piece of the pie she wants. All the work she puts in beforehand will be a huge factor in what "piece" she gets. I will tell you (because I am a proud mama), she has put in the work. All the opportunities she has and is receiving are because she has put in such dedication and such hard work. She sacrificed to reach her long-term goals.

All this made me think about my relationship with Christ. What is your relationship with Jesus like? I am not asking about your church activity; I am asking what kind of relationship do you have with your Lord and savior?

What sacrifices have you made to achieve the long-term goal of being Christ-like? I think we spend our whole lives working for the long-term goal of being Christ-like, and by the time we get close…he takes us home.

Let me start with sacrifices. Sacrifices are anything you give up for his sake—when you die to your flesh to walk in the spirit.

Another way you can tell how your relationship is going is by fruits of the spirit. Paul states in Galatians 5:22–23, "But the fruit of the Spirit is love, joy, peace, forbearance, kindness, goodness, faithfulness, gentleness and self-control." As you grow closer to God, these attributes will grow in you, and others will notice. You will be "moving on up" in your relationship with Christ.

In the Bible, right before Paul states the fruits of the spirit, he issues a stern warning: "The acts of the flesh are obvious: sexual immorality, impurity, and debauchery; idolatry and witchcraft; hatred, discord, jealousy, fits of rage, selfish ambition, dissensions, factions and envy; drunkenness, orgies, and the like" (Galatians 5:19–21).

I know, once again I did not write a "fluffy" message. This is not a judgment by me; this is the "living word" of God. This is information to help you "move on up," so to speak.

I know some want to bark up against me, and that's ok. Don't shoot the messenger. I myself have to make a conscious effort to die to my flesh so I can walk in the spirit. I have lost friends who think I'm weird, 95 percent of the guys I meet don't want to date me, and I struggle just like everyone else. No one is perfect.

However, when love and peace and joy are flowing from you—when your deeds are sincerely kind and you exhibit self-control—there is no feeling like it on Earth. You feel as though you have "moved on up" and you "finally got a piece of the pie."

Going for the Gold

Such an appropriate title during these weeks of the Olympic Games. As I sit and watch these amazing athletes compete, I think of how their whole lives were spent preparing for this moment in time. They train and sacrifice for that one dive, one game, one race, and I am so in awe. The dedication and focus they have is just unbelievable. I love watching the short info segments they do on some of the athletes, how they train and what they have to go through.

Then there is the "agony of defeat," which is heartrending to watch, because, as I said, they work their whole lives for that moment. Just watching Michael Phelps come in second in the two-hundred tonight was agony for me. I can't even imagine how he felt—he was so close!

Where is your dedication and focus? Is there something you have been "training" for your whole life? Have you sacrificed for something? Have you felt the agony of defeat?

I feel my whole life's experience has prepared me for this moment in time. As if God had me in training all these years. I am in a season of life where "all things are working for the good" to glorify God. All I want to do is help others, and the training I have had through the years is all for this moment. Every time I minister to someone, it makes me feel like I have gotten a gold medal. I am blessed. I see the good come from the bad.

Believers are in training. We are being trained to be disciples of Christ. We will have to sacrifice. Every time we die to self, to our flesh, it will feel like a sacrifice. We have to stay focused and dedicated, because when we slip away, things of the world creep in and create havoc in our lives. Fear and anxiety take over, we don't have peace, and we don't feel comforted or protected; you can say we feel the "agony of defeat."

Our goal, "going for gold," is to be transformed in the image of Christ day by day. When we become Christ-like minded, we have strength, we can endure, and we can press on. "We fight *in* the victory not *for* the victory." We don't ever have to experience the "agony of defeat" when we surrender to Jesus. He took on all the agony; he was the sacrifice. "For God so loved the world that he gave his one and only Son, that whoever believes in him shall not perish but have eternal life" (John 3:16).

Jewel of the Nile

I did a message last year at this time called "Diamonds Are a Girl's Best Friend." It seems this is the month I am all about my ladies!!!

This month I am following the theme of that message with "Jewel of the Nile." One of the things I wish for, I pray for, is that every girl and woman could feel like she was a jewel. That she *is* the value. That she *is* the "precious stone."

Always under the microscope (mostly by ourselves), we do not dare to see ourselves as God does. Why is that? When we talk about trusting God for all things, did we ever stop to think that God made us exactly who we are? My nose is just right, my eyes are not too small, and my hair is curly, as it should be. My frame is larger than a skinny girl, and my height is just where it is supposed to be. I mean, if God really created me, then I must be beautiful, right?

When you look in the mirror, what do you see? Do you see a princess? After all, your father is the King. Do you see beauty from within? Peter 3:3 says, "Your beauty should not come from outward adornment such as braided hair, gold jewelry and fine clothes. Instead it should be that of your inner self, the unfading beauty of a gentle and sweet spirit, which is of great worth to God." Did you read that last part? *Which is of great worth to God.*

I urge us to speak only good things about ourselves. Let's talk about how fabulous we each are. Encourage, uplift, and edify: those are the three words we need to practice on ourselves. It hurts my heart to hear women, especially those that are close to me, talk so poorly about themselves. To allow people to treat them poorly, and for them not to realize what value they have. What value they bring to their families, friendships, and even their workplaces. When we have low self-esteem or do not know we are valuable, we will wind up in relationships that are very unhealthy. We will stay in them longer than we should. We will allow others to take our joy and crush our spirit.

It does not matter where you have come from or what kind of acceptance you had in life. Once you become a believer, the "old is gone and the new is here." You enter into an inheritance, into the royal family; you go from rags to riches in an instant. You become the princess. I know that sounds like a fairy tale, but I assure you it is not. The love of Christ can change you. It transforms you, it builds you up, it gives you strength to endure, and it gives you a solid rock to stand on for all of your life. And then, when it's all over, your seat in heaven awaits you.

Something I encourage some of the women I counsel is to write out positive things about themselves on Post-It notes and put them on their bathroom mirrors. Reprogram your mind to who you really are in Christ. God never makes a mistake. He "knit you together" just as you were meant to be, a rare and precious jewel.

Love Is in the Air

February, the month of love. Valentine's Day is the holiday of love. If you have a spouse or a mate, it's a great day. You get some chocolates and some lovey gifts, and your mate expresses through cards how much he or she loves you. Love is in the air. You feel it all around you; every store has Valentine's Day decorations.

What about the people that do not have a spouse or a mate? It can be a lonely day. It can be a day that reminds you just how alone you are. Even if you hang out with your girlfriends or your fellows, you still know you don't have a mate, yes? And those that say, "Oh, it's just another day, it doesn't bother me at all"—I don't believe you. We were made for relationships. God intended us to be matched up. That is why he gave Adam a helpmate...Eve.

Sometimes I wonder: If what I said above is really true, why does God leave some of us alone for such long periods of time? Today, January 26, would have been my twenty-second wedding anniversary. On one hand I am sad, and on the other hand not. I love marriage and all it stands for, and I love to love. My heart is so big and so full. Kind of odd, since I grew up feeling so unloved and unlovable. But God gave me this extraordinary gift—to love like it's never going to hurt. So I am excited about the person God is molding for me, and I am waiting on him to bring the man fourth.

The sad part for me is that I didn't wait on the Lord twenty-two years ago. I did what I wanted to do. I tucked away all the red flags and made a free-will choice that had many consequences. For me, for him, and for our daughter. Today we are all still family and in a very good place. My ex and I do have love for one another. Different than before; I think better than before. That is the power of God: "all things work for the good." This was a long time coming and a long time waiting.

As I think about February and Valentine's Day, I do feel the "oh I wish I had a valentine of my own" thing, but I also know that I am loved. I know I have this love from God that is unshakeable, unmovable. He wants what is best for me every minute of every day. That fills me. It takes away the waiting.

I do not always wait on the Lord. My flesh takes over, and I want to be in the driver's seat. I hate being a passenger! But I am learning to sit back and relax. I am learning to let "Jesus take the wheel." When I do that, I always wind up at a much better destination. When I take the wheel...*geez*....I wind up on a dirt road, alone, in the dark, and afraid.

I want to share the lyrics to a song by The David Crowder Band. When I hear this song and I think about who God is and how he loves me...my feelings of loneliness are gone. The waiting is ok. And in February, when love is in the air and everything is Valentine's...I have the greatest love of all, and God fills me.

"How He Loves Us" by The David Crowder Band
(I take out *us* and I always put in *ME*—and
sing from the bottom of who I am)

He is jealous for me,
Loves like a hurricane, I am a tree,
Bending beneath the weight of his wind and mercy.
When all of a sudden,
I am unaware of these afflictions, eclipsed by glory,
And I realize just how beautiful you are,
And how great your affections are for me.

And oh, how he loves me, oh,
Oh, how he loves me,
How he loves me

And I am his portion and he is my prize,
Drawn to redemption by the grace in his eyes,
If grace is an ocean, we're all sinking.
So heaven meets earth like an unforeseen kiss,
And my heart turns violently inside of my chest,
I don't have time to maintain these regrets,
When I think about the way...

He loves me,
Oh, how he loves me.

Memories

Today is March 2. I did not realize till my daughter reminded me that I am two years cancer and treatment free. Today two years ago was the last day of my treatment. How easily we forget. You would think such a tough period in time would remain longer in one's memory, but honestly I can't remember the sickness. I do, however, remember the blessings. The blessings from that terrible time stay with me so vividly. So much more than the treatments.

I have a sister in Christ who is going through breast cancer now. I tell you, she is an amazing woman of God. Her faith and trust in him is so strong it takes your breath away. I just read her posting on *Caring Bridge* before I sat down to write. I can tell it is overwhelming for her, but she is shining such a bright light of how she is trusting God. Although she is human and feeling all that's going on, she has her eyes in the right place.

I think we all have had times that were so overwhelming, so devastating to us that it was hard to catch our breath. Where did you turn? Where did you look for comfort? Were you a believer at that time or not? If you were a believer, did you trust God, and did he come through for you?

It is so easy to trust God when things are going well. When no one is sick. When no one is lonely. When your children are fine and a paycheck is coming. We tend to thank God for the blessings, tithe a little more, and go about our business. But when it starts raining, when that storm comes and the dark clouds have arrived…how much do you trust him? Is that trust noticeable to others? Trusting God in a storm is like shining a flashlight in a dark tunnel. Those coming from a distance can see the light, and those around you see it brightly. My friend, the one going through cancer, is shining a bright light. I hope you know that, dear sister.

As I said earlier, as I look back on my own journey—not just cancer but all the heartache, the struggles, the dark tunnels—they do not seem so terrible. Those memories don't have any feeling to them. What I do feel, the memories that are rooted in my soul, is that God never left me. That God's love encompassed my mind, body, and soul. That hope and faith are in my every breath. That because he gave his son for my sin, because his son shed his blood for me, I will have life ever after. And that while I am here on this Earth I will have peace that truly surpasses all understanding, and I will have strength to endure anything that comes my way.

My small group and I are doing a book study: *Traveling Light*, by Max Lucado. This past week I encouraged my ladies to wake up every day with "The Lord is my shepherd; I shall not want." I thought if we really felt that—got that under our skin and imbedded into every part of our being—we would live in a way that God intended us to: content, joyful, and fearless. As I look back on this anniversary date, I can really see how true that statement is.

Please read each line of Psalm 23, and listen to what David was really saying. Although it's often cited when someone dies,

I feel this is a psalm to live by each and every day. I made some notes beside the lyrics, expressing what I get out of it.

The Lord is my shepherd, I shall not want. *I have everything I need because he is my keeper.*
He makes me lie down in green pastures. *He knows when I need rest and makes a place for me to do that.*
He leads me beside still waters, he restores my soul. *He knows when I am thirsty and weary, and he fills me.*
He leads me in paths of righteousness for his name's sake. *He makes a lighted path for me to follow that I can't possibly miss.*
Even though I walk through the valley of the shadow of death, I fear no evil; for thou art with me; thy rod and thy staff, they comfort me. *I will walk through dark places, but I need not fear; he never leaves me, his hands surround me, and he breathes his peace upon me in all situations.*
Thou prepares a table before me in the presence of my enemies. *I am royalty, and there is a seat with my name for all those to see.*
Thou anoints my head with oil, my cup overflows. *I am marked forever, and I will always be filled to the brim with blessings.*
Surely goodness and mercy shall follow me all the days of my life, and I shall dwell in the house of the Lord forever. *His grace and his mercy are never ending, and when I am no longer in this life, I will meet my savior and have eternal life with him.*

The State of Relationships

Are you married? If so, how is that relationship? As a woman, do you submit to your husband? Do you honor and respect him? Do you appreciate the little things? If you're a man, do you love your wife like Jesus loved the church? (That one doesn't even need anything after it, does it?)

Parents, how is your relationship with your kids? Have you put in the time and now are reaping the benefits? Have you spent more time on your dreams and your life, leaving your children on the back burner?

Employees, how are your relationships at work? Do you stay to yourself, or do you find moments to engage with others? Bosses, do you let your employees know how much you appreciate all they do to help you succeed?

Are your friendships growing? Are you nurturing? Are you giving as much as you're taking? Boyfriends and girlfriends, are you staying for fear of being alone, even though you know he or she is not the one? Are you helping each other grow and develop?

Those are a lot of questions, aren't they? Relationships are the most important thing in life, in my opinion. My pastor just did a sermon on spending our time wisely. I was in tune with what he was saying, because I have always felt that good relationships need time. Not time as in hours and days but as in *our time*, to give of oneself, our own time and space.

My daughter, at almost twenty-three, still likes to hang out with me and comes home whenever she can. We talk daily. She tells me things and shares her life, and we are in a season now were the mother-daughter thing is moving into friendship. The other night we sat in my car in the pouring rain and talked for a long while. Both sharing intimate things about our own personal lives. I was reaping what I sowed. My parents used to say to me when my daughter was younger, "Your whole life is your child." (Mind you, this came from two people who abandoned their children.) My thoughts then and now are, "That's right!" I am so glad I gave my everything to that relationship. I sacrificed and put her needs above my own, because I had a small window (yes, in raising kids you get a small window of time) to nurture, teach, share, and speak into her life. When she went to college, I wasn't even sure what I was going to do with all my time. But God worked it all out, and the benefits of giving all that time to her growth were so worth it.

Relationships also need forgiveness, mercy, and grace. We need to reconcile when the relationship takes a turn for the worse. Now I know this sounds easy, but so many of us, including myself, would rather let an important relationship fall to the wayside then take the first step, be the bigger person—especially if we feel we did nothing wrong.

"Leave your gift there before the altar, and go your way. First *be reconciled* to your brother, and then come and offer your gift" (Matthew 5:24). That was the Bible verse in my devotional on January 17. Now, every year on that day I read the same verse, because I go through my devotionals year after year; I always learn something new. On this day it always seems I have a relationship I need to address. This year it was my older brother. This is a difficult relationship. I love him so much, but he is a very difficult person to get along with. A little over a month ago, we had a big falling out. He was explosive and told me, "Lose my number. I'm deleting yours. Never want to talk to you ever again." I tried to tell him he didn't mean that, and he insisted he did.

A couple of weeks later, I sent him a picture on the day of my daughter's graduation and said, "I miss you and love you, wish you were here." No response. Couple of weeks later, on Christmas, I sent a text: "Love you, Merry Christmas." Still no response. New Year's: no response.

So I thought to myself and said out loud, "I'm at peace. I did all I could. Can't help it if he doesn't want to talk to me. I'm done." (I did feel bad, though.) I tried to act like it didn't bother me, but it did. So I was concentrating on moving on... until January 17, when I read that Bible verse.

BE RECONCILED. That's what I heard. Not "*try* to be reconciled." *BE* reconciled. Loud and clear, God was telling me I had to go back and attempt again.

Now, can I just say God and I have had these moments before? He says, "Just DO IT," and I say, "Really, why am I

always the one that has to make the move?" And his answer is, "Because I said so."

So I sent my brother an e-mail and told him I loved him, I missed him, and if what I said had hurt him, I was sorry and wanted him to be part of my life. I didn't want to send that e-mail. Not that I didn't love my brother, but how many times am I supposed to try? "Then Peter came to Jesus and asked, 'Lord how many times shall I forgive my brother when he sins against me? Up to seven times?' Jesus answered, 'I tell you, not seven times but seventy-seven times'" (Matthew 18:21–22).

I did receive a response. It started with "I love you and always will."

I am so glad God is persistent with me. The state of that relationship is good, and I am grateful for that.

So I ask you, Is there a relationship that needs mending? Is there a relationship that is important to you, but you're allowing pride and ego to keep you from reaching out? *BE* reconciled. It's ok to make the first move and give a hand of mercy, grace, and forgiveness. What you will find in return is freedom, peace, and restoration.

What Are You Armed With?

This month I was stumped. I was not sure what I should write about. November 1, 2, and 3 came and went, and I still had no message. There is so much going on in the world today, I just did not know where to begin. On one hand I wanted to write about trusting God and how worry, fear, and anxiety can destroy us, and then on the other hand I wanted to write about comfort and peace in the midst of horrific situations like the LAX shooting. Things here on Earth are really exploding. It seems weekly some random person is killing others. Politics have caused so much strife, separation, hatred, and anger. I don't ever recall it being like this.

My friend and I were talking about something the other day, and he referred to a "spiritual bubble." That stuck with me, and all I could think about was that I want to be in a spiritual bubble with Jesus and never come out. (I would like to take a few people—and my poodle—with me in that bubble, though.)

Truth is, we need all of those messages, right? We need to arm ourselves with truth about worry and fear. About peace that surpasses our human nature. This Bible verse is what came to me, and it is so powerful: "Do not be anxious about anything, but in every situation, by prayer and petition, with thanksgiving, present your requests to God. And the peace of God, which transcends all understanding, will guard your hearts and your minds in Christ Jesus" (Philippians 4:6).

Do you arm yourself with that truth? What do you tell yourself in the midst of worry and fear? When anxiety has covered you, what do you do? Where do you turn? The Bible tells us we do not need to be anxious for ANYTHING. In EVERY situation we can bring our request to God, and HIS peace, which TRANCENDS ALL HUMAN UNDERSTANDING, will guard our hearts and minds in Jesus.

WOW. Marinate on that for a bit. Really read and soak that up. That would be all the ammunition you would need.

To me...that's my spiritual bubble. That is what I am clinging to, getting inside of when the world around me is falling apart. For those of you with children, especially young children, you must teach them truth. You have to show them how you arm yourself when tough times come around. Imagine for one minute if you were raised your whole life on the Bible verse above. Every time you came home with a problem, a concern, a worry a fear, even a death in the family, your parents or parent wrote this out for you. Said it out loud to you. It was second nature. What would that look like for you now as an adult? Do you think it would change the way you handle situations?

Let me leave you with this: there is freedom when you can give everything to your heavenly father. Just like when you were a little kid (well, for most of us). You didn't have any burdens; they rested all upon your mother and/or father.

What Course Are You On?

"In his heart a man plans his course, but he the Lord determines his steps" (Proverbs 16:9).

What is your course? Do you have a plan? In your life right now, what are you hopeful for? Wanting? Needing?

I was restless last night. I kept waking up and planning my course. Yep, I sure was. I didn't realize that was what I was doing until this morning, just now, when I read that verse above. I wanted answers *now* to something. I wanted to know right now what was going to be. My heart already was planning the course. I was praying and asking God what to do. I first was going to reach out to a friend, but it just didn't feel right. And on top of that I heard that friend's voice: "Have you taken it to God?"

I told my friend that, and then he told me, "Look for a Bible verse that speaks to your request." At first I thought, "Should I just start googling? Open and close the Bible?" So I didn't do anything. I went about my morning and did my devotional. Didn't hear God speaking. I then recited my own twenty-minute message. Still nothing. And then I did my Bible study for small group, on Ester. Went to the questions on what I studied, and it told me to read Proverbs 16:9—and there was my answer!

I can plan in my heart. I can pray and even bring my request, my desires, to the Lord, but it is he who ultimately determines my steps.

So where are you heading? What steps has God put before you? Are you enjoying the walk or hurrying it up? I was hurrying it up. I was not basking in the stroll of it, enjoying the scenery. I was running up the steps to get to the top as quick as I could. The trouble with that is I will miss so much along the way.

It is hard to wait on the Lord. We are in a supersonic age—everything is at our fingertips. Fast and easy. But fast and easy is not always good. It's good if you're in a hurry to get dinner on the table, but when you're planning your life, when it's your future hopes and dreams at hand...Fast and easy? Not good. Slow and steady, that's the way to go.

God has got you. He knows all things. It's ok if you get impatient. Learn from that. Just take one step at a time. Savor each flight of stairs, breathe at each landing—look behind you at how far you have come. Enjoy the view. Trust me, when you get to the top, when God takes you to the top, it will be all it is supposed to be. May not be what you expected, but the journey up there will be so worth it.

Everyday Life

I thought this month I would write about everyday life. Everyday life is not always pretty, is it? It seems we go from the mountaintop highs to the valley lows. Standing in the valley just seems to last longer than standing on the mountaintop. Do you think that is really so, or do you think it is our perspective?

My everyday life these days has me in the valley. My dad is dying as I write this; he is in hospice and just has days to live. He went from being in apparently good health in March of this year to having stage 4 lung cancer, with a brain tumor, and only days to live. One of my dearest and oldest friends is about to have a double mastectomy. And just after I got used to the fact that my daughter went off to college, she's coming home for the summer.

I guess I need to explain that one so you don't get the wrong idea. I adore my child. I only have one, and she is so precious to me. I had such a hard time when she left to go to college. I felt alone and abandoned. I knew that was not what was going on, but because I was abandoned as a child, certain things trigger that feeling of abandonment. God and I worked together, and he was as faithful as he always is. Now I have a whole new life outside of being my daughter's mom. So just as I got used to this new season in life…I get to go through it all again—happy to see her come home, and then sad she will yet again have to leave.

I talk to my best friend daily. She is my "person." I have two of those friends. I have been blessed with friends that have been with me for years, but I have two people I talk to a lot. This friend, she is my everyday buddy. I can tell her anything, and when I say anything, I am so glad no one ever overhears us. She is such a spiritual person, so grounded in the word and her relationship with her heavenly father. Her attitude is amazing. We laugh and joke about new boobies and new bodies, and I never feel her being anxious or nervous. But sometimes, when I am sitting alone, I think about my friend and what she is going to go through. How if anything happened to her what a great loss that would be for me. This is a person that liked me and accepted me when I was a very young girl and I felt very unlovable and alone. This is a person that accepted me exactly for who I was at every stage of my life. The love I have for her is so deep and so strong, and I sometimes feel fearful of not having her here with me to continue life.

What Kind of Coverage Do you Have?

Insurance policies seem so overrated at times, don't you think? You pay all this money so that if the worst happens, you're covered. Nine out of ten times, the worst never happens, right?

I pay about $3,000 a year to have insurance on my car and my daughter's car. We have all the coverage one needs and then a few extras, "just in case." I have to have this coverage—by law, and also because I want to make sure if the worst happens, they got me covered. The thing is, the worst has not happened. I am making "deposits" and getting nothing in return. I mean, I guess the assurance is something. I have the assurance that if I get in an accident, I'm covered. I got peace of mind.

Health insurance is outrageous. Costs me money, costs my company money, and then when I go to the doctor, I still have copays and deductibles. But I need it, can't be without it, because if the worst happens, the cost could cripple me. House insurance is not as expensive, but if I'm not protected, a disaster could cripple me in many ways as well.

So my car, house, and health are covered, right? What about my soul? What about my state of mind? Where is the insurance policy for that? Do you think there is one? Wouldn't it be nice to know that in times of crisis, in times of emotional breakdown, in times of death, cancer, loss of job, loss of friends, in times of the world falling down around you, there is an insurance policy? One that covers everything? What would the cost of that be, do you think? Do you think there is an insurance policy that could cover everything that could ever go wrong in your life? Every trial, every fear, every anxiety, every disappointment, every letdown, every heartbreak...What kind of policy could there be?

I am so glad you asked that question. Wait a minute. I asked the question, didn't I? And I have the answer: "The Way." That is the name of the policy. "I am the way, the truth and the life. No one comes to the father except through me" (John 14:6). It cost one his son; it costs you faith. It costs you the faith of a mustard seed, the smallest seed there is. That's it! Want to know what it covers? Whoooo-hoooo! It's the best coverage you can get. No deductible, no out-of-pocket expenses, and no copays. Here are a few things it covers:

- **FEAR** "For I am the Lord, your God, who takes hold of your right hand and says to you, do not fear, I will help you" (Isaiah 41:13).
- **ANXIETY** "Do not be anxious about anything, but in everything, by prayer and petition, with thanksgiving present your requests to God" (Philippians 4:6).
- **HEARTBREAK** "He heals the brokenhearted and binds up their wounds" (Psalm 147:3).
- **LONELINESS** "I am with you and will watch over you wherever you go" (Genesis 28:15).
- **COMFORT** "Come to me, all you who are weary and burdened, and I will give you rest" (Matthew 11:20).

- **COURAGE** "He gives strength to the weary and increases the power of the weak" (Isaiah 40:29).
- **DEATH** "Even though I walk through the valley of the shadow of death, I will fear no evil, for you are with me, your rod and your staff, they comfort me" (Psalm 23:4).

I think this covers everything in the worst-case scenario, yes? And I want to give you one more, one that covers anything I may have left out, anything that may pop up:

- **PEACE** "Peace I leave with you; my peace I give you. I do not give to you as the world gives. Do not let your hearts be troubled and do not be afraid" (John 14:27).

I picked PEACE as the final one, the be-all, because the truth is, we cannot control our circumstance, but we can control our response. We have a choice where to turn, what coverage to take, what policy to invest in. The Bible tells us, in Philippians 4:7, "And the peace of God, which transcends *all understanding*, will guard your hearts and minds in Christ Jesus." I am a witness that this promise is true.

I have had a rough six weeks. So thankful I have The Way policy. In my last newsletter, I mentioned my dad became ill and then passed away, all within two months. I have been ill with a severe sinus infection for more than three weeks. Pharmacy filled the wrong prescription, had two rounds of steroids and three rounds of antibiotics, and I'm still sick. And if that was not enough, I found a lump in my breast and was just told the other day that it's 99.9 percent likely I have breast cancer. Stage 1 most likely, and will have to have surgery regardless.

I need coverage, don't you think? I need a promise, and I need a guarantee that, no matter what, I am going to be ok. I need peace of mind. I need a spirit that is uplifting and encouraging in the midst of all this "stuff."

I took out my policy many years ago. The minute I was saved. The minute I gave my life to Christ. However, I didn't believe all the coverage. I didn't trust that the policy would do as it said. Took me years to get to a place where I had the peace of mind I have with my other insurance policies. Today, though, I am covered, and I have peace that surpasses all understanding.

If you knew the old me, that statement in itself is HUGE. I was the one who wanted a guarantee of everything, and I wanted to control everything. I didn't have peace about anything. But today my spirit is calm. I have faith and trust that all will be ok. I know I am not in charge, and I have learned to look at the blessings within my circumstances. My thoughts these days are, "Cara, this is another opportunity to shine a light, another opportunity to show what a believer does in times of crisis." We look up—that is what we do. We turn to The Way policy, the promises that God has given, to never leave, never forsake. To never be worried or anxious. To be thankful in all things. That joy comes from the Lord, not our circumstances. The biggest promise, the greatest thing about The Way policy...If the worst case happens, I go home; I have a place waiting for me in heaven. My future is secure. I have eternal life. What insurance policy can give you that? What material thing here on Earth can give you that? What human can guarantee to never leave you, never forsake you?

So I ask you, what kind of coverage do you have? Do you know where you're going when it's all over? Where will you turn when life throws you a bump—or a boulder—in the road?

I invite you to "The Way" policy, to surrender all you have been carrying. You were never meant to carry the burden, walk the walk alone. Jesus invites you into a personal relationship with him. He invites you to believe. He asks you to have faith—only a mustard seed—and to trust him. That deposit reaps abundant life. That is what you get in return: give him your life, and he will give you eternal life.

Cuts and Infections

H ave you ever been cooking or tinkering with something and cut yourself? It looks deep, but you rinse it with water, pour some peroxide in it, stick a butterfly Band-Aid on it, and off you go. It looks like it may be getting better, but it's not. You notice it is red around the edges even though it is closed up. You can see something is very wrong. You *feel* something is wrong. You go to the doctor, and he tells you that you have an infection and he needs to cut it open to clean it up so he can stitch it properly. OH MY GOSH!!! Now that is going to hurt, isn't it? Oh, and I forgot to tell you: there will be no anesthesia. I would be screaming, and if I knew about the lack of anesthesia before I went to the doctor, I may not have even gone.

They cut it open, clean it up, stitch it, and send you home. You are in so much pain you can't believe this happened from such a small thing like cutting your finger. It was not hurting like this when you first arrived at the doctor's office. You thought something might be wrong, all did not seem well, but you were not in this kind of pain. How can this be? After a few days, you notice it does not hurt as much. It's starting to heal. A few days ago there was no way that you would have believed that you would feel better, because to you they may as well have cut your finger off. You heave a sigh of relief, you feel better, your finger can move more freely, and you are so glad you took care of it. Sometimes the cut leaves a scar. I don't even know why people have scars—maybe as a reminder of sorts. But the wound, the cut, is clean, it's healed.

This is how it is on the inside as well. The soul can become infected, by a harsh word, emotional abuse, or physical abuse. An event that took place as a child and was tucked away by your little mind. You tried to put a Band-Aid on it with alcohol, drugs, or even food. You did all kinds of things to avoid feeling the pain. I know there are cuts that are so deep and so infected they hurt you every day. The last thing you want to do is talk about it. For some of you, the pain is so much you think that not being here may be better, because then you would not have to feel this unbearable thing that is aching your soul.

I understand. I have never experienced not wanting to be in this world, but I have been hurt so bad it brought me to my knees.

There was a time when I was scared to talk about my infections. I was afraid I would find something I didn't like, and that would be terrible, because I already hated myself. What else could I possibly find out? I was scared, and I didn't want to go back in order to go forward. I didn't want to find out I had some other "infection" I did not know was there. But God knows it's there, and he wants to clean it up. I know you don't want him to touch it; it's painful. But you must trust him. He will be careful. He knows when it's time to open you up, to reopen that wound you have been putting Band-Aids on for a long time. Allow him to work in you. He is the best doctor there is. If you're crying, it's good. If you feel it hurts, it's ok. Peroxide burns on a cut that is infected. Today it will hurt, and tomorrow it may even feel worse, but I *assure* you, in a little while you will feel better. Allow him to work in you.

God does not want you to walk through life with cuts and infections in your soul. He created you just the way you are. "Fearfully and wonderfully made." Your character will be transformed. Your cuts as they heal will shape and mold your character to help others to be free of the pain and suffering that comes from cuts left unattended. The work that God does in you will be life changing, not just for you but for others as you shine a bright light. "Your word is a lamp to my feet and a light for my path" (Psalm 119:105).

As I was gathering this passage, I saw on-line this next quote—how awesome!—and had to share it: "*God's Word, like a lamp, illuminates. It helps us discern spiritual danger so we can avoid it, and points us in the right direction to take our lives. It lights the path we take through life.*"

It's hard to go back in time, especially when you can feel the tension and anxiety creeping up. It's the fear of the unknown, and I know it's scary. But fear is False Evidence Appearing Real. Write that down and carry it with you every day.

Here are a few Bible verses I carry with me all the time. I have copies in my purse, at work, and at home. A reminder that I do not need to be afraid.

- "God is my refuge and strength, an ever present help in trouble" (Psalm 46:1).
- "Peace I leave with you, my peace I give you. I do not give to you as the world gives. Do not let your hearts be troubled and do not be afraid" (John 14:27).
- "For I am the Lord your God, who takes hold of your right hand and says to you, do not be afraid, I will help you" (Isaiah 41:13).

Do you have cuts that have been left unattended? Are there some infections way down deep, but you are too afraid to let anyone look at them? Do not be discouraged. I know it's hard. I know it is not easy to lie down and allow someone to open up your cut and pour peroxide in there. You have to close your eyes and imagine that God is doing the pouring. He is pouring in grace and mercy, love and forgiveness, and strength to do all things. "I can do all things in Christ who strengthens me" (Philippians 4:13). He will not forsake you or leave you. He will hold your hand, and you can squeeze it as tight as you need to when it burns really bad.

"I will not forget you. See, I have inscribed you on the palms of my hands" (Isaiah 49:15–16).

PeepHoles and the Big Lens

An instant camera has a tiny little peephole to look through, right? It gets you a decent picture—not the best, but good enough. The big, beautiful camera with the huge lens and all the gadgets? You see such a clear shot and the picture comes out better, right? I think we can all agree a Kodak instant camera does the job—it takes the picture—but the Canon Rebel, let's say, does a better job—you get top-quality pictures, yes?

When we look at our lives through a peephole, we see a picture. Not a big picture, a little blurry. We have a feeling it will come out ok, but we are not certain. When we look through the lens that God sees, the BIG picture, the outcome is so much better.

But how do we get to that point? To the point where we are looking through the lens that God wants us to? Truth is, when our circumstances start to shake us, it seems we immediately look through the peephole when in fact that is the exact time we should look through the "God" lens.

I think it has to do with trust. Do we really trust him? I mean do you *really* trust him? In all things? For me, I have had to really examine this question over the last several months. I had to really ask myself, "Cara, do you really trust God to take care of everything?" When things are going good, when my circumstances don't seem to overwhelm me, my answer is a resounding YES!!! In the past, when my circumstances overwhelmed me, I thought, "Let me give him a hand, I'm sure he needs my help." Disaster, that's what I got. My circumstances seemed worse, even though they weren't. I was worse. I was anxious and fearful and just kept trying to control it.

I have to use my breast cancer experience as an example, because those are my circumstances these days. On Monday, one and a half weeks after surgery, I was feeling great. I was thinking, "This is a walk in the park. I know I have to have radiation, but if that's it, that's all, with some extra meds over the years…how great is this?" I trusted God, and it all came out good. I at moments almost forgot I had cancer…until Wednesday. On Wednesday I spent five hours at the cancer center with doctors and talked about chemo, radiation, scans, and the 29 percent chance that ONE cancer cell escaped. Imagine that! They could tell me there was a 29 percent chance that ONE cancer cell escaped and may be somewhere in my body. I also found out that my Jewish heritage could possibly put me at risk for a few other issues as well.

I think the last thing I was thinking with all that info was, "Now, Cara, don't forget to trust God in all things." I was thinking, "Aren't Jews God's chosen people?" I was laughing, trying to make a joke. What I was really thinking was "This is not a walk in the park," and there was no mistaking it: I had cancer.

I closed up any lens I was looking through, and all I had left was an instant camera. I could not see beyond the blur in the peephole. Where was my trust now? I was overwhelmed with fear.

I knew that if I didn't put ALL my trust in God, I was not going to make it through this ordeal. I was powerless, and all I had was my trust in Him. I knew that, but how was I going to accomplish it?

I cried out to the Lord, told him how afraid I was and how I needed him, and asked him to please give me a word, give me a sign, give me something to hold on to. Here is the word I received: "Going a little farther, he fell with his face to the ground and prayed, 'My father, if it is possible, may this cup be taken from me. Yet not as I will, but as you will'" (from the story of Jesus in Gethsemane, Matthew 26:39).

Now, I have to take a moment to say my initial reaction was, "This is your word to me?!!!" I wanted to give the word back. All I heard was NO, not taking away your cup.

The Bible tells us "he was afraid and overwhelmed with sorrow." Jesus was AFRAID? Just like me, just like you. But *he* trusted God's will. He did not like his circumstances at all. Not only did he not like them but he even knew what was ahead. We usually don't like our circumstances, and we don't even know what is ahead.

But Jesus trusted God enough. He knew to look through the lens of his father, and he became the King, the savior of the world! He did suffer, just like we all will at some time in our lives, but we will never suffer like Christ did. Christ had to be separated from God for a moment so that we would have eternal life, yet we never will be separated from God.

God did not let Jesus down. God will not let those that believe down either. I can put my trust in God, because he will never forsake me, no matter what. "Those who know your name will trust in you, for you Lord have never forsaken those who see you" (Psalm 9:10).

It took me a day or two to accept my "cup." I kept asking him, "Are you sure?" and he kept saying yes. Over the next couple of days, I received a package in the mail from the mother of a woman I met only ONE time. I received a gift card from someone I don't get to see or talk to often. What I felt as I looked and read the notes and card was my heavenly father telling me, "I love you, I have not left you, I will not forsake you, I am right here." I was able to throw out the instant camera and zoom in with the big lens.

I know that my picture is going to be bright and perfect in every way when it is fully developed.

Are You Willing to Jump into the Fire?

I love the show *LA Ink*. For those that do not know, it is a reality show about Kat Von D. She is a tattoo artist with a shop in Hollywood, California. The part I love about this show is the stories behind the people who come in and get tattoos. I know some people tend to judge people who are covered in tattoos; some people even think it's against God. I really don't get caught up in all that. What I know is these people, real people who come into her shop, have the most amazing stories and tattoos.

One guy came in to get "Daniel in the lion's den" tattooed across his back. He had never before had a tattoo, and when Corey asked him why he would get such a huge tattoo and what it meant to him, this was his response:

> I am a fireman, and I run into burning buildings all the time. Daniel is a character from the Old Testament in the Bible, and he was thrown into the lion's den to die. Daniel had unbelievable faith in his God, and he knew that God was with him no matter what. When the soldiers opened the lion's cage at dawn, there was Daniel, unharmed. Not a scratch. I wanted

to get this tattoo as a reminder that every time I
run into a burning building, I never have to be
afraid, because God is with me.

I was wrecked. I immediately had to go and read the book
of Daniel, because in all these years as a believer, I had never
read that book. Not only was there the story of the lion's den
but also the story of three Jewish men who were thrown into
the fire and were untouched by the flames. Three men—
Shadrach, Meshach, and Abednego—were thrown into a furnace and they were UNTOUCHED.

Daniel in the lion's den is an amazing story, and I encourage you to read it (or maybe we can look at that next month).
But I want to focus on the three Jews and their unbelievable
trust and faith in God.

I am going to write out some of the passages from the book
of Daniel because they are so powerful and almost unbelievable I don't want you to miss anything. Here we go:

"You have issued a decree, O king, that everyone
who hears the sound of the horn, flute, zither,
lyre, harp, pipes and all kinds of music must fall
down and worship the image of gold, and that
whoever does not fall down and worship will be
thrown into a blazing furnace. But there are
some Jews whom you have set over the affairs of
the province of Babylon—Shadrach, Meshach
and Abednego—who pay no attention to you, O
king. They neither serve your gods nor worship
the image of gold you have set up." Furious with
rage, Nebuchadnezzar summoned Shadrach,

Meshach, and Abednego. So these men were brought before the king, and Nebuchadnezzar said to them, "Is it true, Shadrach, Meshach, and Abednego, that you do not serve my gods or worship the image of gold I have set up? Now when you hear the sound of the horn, flute, zither, lyre, harp, pipes, and all kinds of music, if you are ready to fall down and worship the image I made, very good. But if you do not worship it, you will be thrown immediately into a blazing furnace. Then what god will be able to rescue you from my hand?"

Shadrach, Meshach, and Abednego replied to the king, "O Nebuchadnezzar, we do not need to defend ourselves before you in this matter. If we are thrown into the blazing furnace, the God we serve is able to save us from it, and he will rescue us from your hand, O king. But even if he does not, we want you to know, O king, that we will not serve your gods or worship the image of gold you have set up."

Then Nebuchadnezzar was furious with Shadrach, Meshach and Abednego, and his attitude toward them changed. He ordered the furnace heated seven times hotter than usual and commanded some of the strongest soldiers in his army to tie up Shadrach, Meshach and Abednego and throw them into the blazing furnace. So these men, wearing their robes, trousers, turbans and other clothes, were bound and thrown into the blazing furnace.

The king's command was so urgent and the furnace so hot that the flames of the fire killed the soldiers who took up Shadrach, Meshach and Abednego, and these three men, firmly tied, fell into the blazing furnace.

Then King Nebuchadnezzar leaped to his feet in amazement and asked his advisers, "Weren't there three men that we tied up and threw into the fire?" They replied, "Certainly, O king." He said, "Look! I see four men walking around in the fire, unbound and unharmed, and the fourth looks like a son of the gods." Nebuchadnezzar then approached the opening of the blazing furnace and shouted, "Shadrach, Meshach and Abednego, servants of the Most High God, come out! Come here!" So Shadrach, Meshach and Abednego came out of the fire, and the satraps, prefects, governors and royal advisers crowded around them. They saw that the fire had not harmed their bodies, nor was a hair of their heads singed; their robes were not scorched, and there was no smell of fire on them. Then Nebuchadnezzar said, "Praise be to the God of Shadrach, Meshach and Abednego, who has sent his angel and rescued his servants! They trusted in him and defied the king's command and were willing to give up their lives rather than serve or worship any god except their own God.

I know you're thinking, "This cannot be true." I had to read it a few times myself. First I had to say, "Cara, if you believe the

Bible is God's living word, then, as unbelievable as it may seem, the story is true." And then I asked myself, "Would I get into the fire and trust God?"

I know some of you are new in your walk and may still be unsure of whom you worship. So let's focus on the trust part. Truth is, you have many furnaces in life, yes? Many times where you have to go into it or through it. No passing Go; you have to jump, yes? How do you make it through? What do you believe in, trust in, have faith in?

How awesome would it be to have the faith and the trust that the three Jews had to make this statement with such confidence? *"If we are thrown into the blazing furnace, the God we serve is able to save us from it, and he will rescue us from your hand, O king."* Imagine if you had that thought when you went to the job interview, took that final, received the results of your CT scan, or approached a breakup, illness, or even death.

I know that sometimes you do think that way, and then your furnace burns you. Right? Then you lose hope and faith, because you think God did not hear you or was not there for you. That is very hard to absorb and makes you not want to get burned again. The other part here is that the three Jews also said, *"But even if he does not, we want you to know, O king, that we will not serve your gods or worship the image of gold you have set up."* Meaning they trusted God no matter what the outcome. Sometimes you will get burned, but what you cannot see is the other side and the good that God will bring out of that trial. Every prayer is not always answered as we would like, because that prayer was not according to God's will. Key word—*God's* will. When you grow a relationship with God, with Jesus, your thoughts and prayers start to align with *his* will for your life.

And what happens is, when the fire is before you, you will have confidence to jump, even though you don't want to. You will trust that no matter if you get burned or not, God is with you, just like in the furnace ("there were four..."). He will protect you, give you strength to endure, never forsake you, and he will make all things good for those that love him.

Troubled Times

We are in troubled times. I have friends going through stuff, and my heart feels for them. I myself am going through tough times, and sometimes the road seems so narrow I wonder if I will fit.

In a time when the economy is failing, children are starving, people are losing their possessions, kids are killing each other and themselves, parents are consumed by everything but their kids, courts battle about same-sex marriage, and cancer and sickness is everywhere, I would say the world is a mess—a big, fat mess.

Man has made a mess of this world. This is not the world God had in mind. He wanted us to live in a perfect world without sin, and now we are in a world that is run by sin. Thank goodness God loved us so much he offered us salvation...his SON.

Some people find it hard to believe and have faith during times of trial. Some people abandon what they believe because they think that God has forsaken them. I can assure you he has not.

God is bigger than anything you can imagine. We keep thinking he is somehow human. Yes, we do. If we understood the magnitude of who he is, of how powerful he is, we would stand on solid rock. "On Christ the solid rock I stand; all other ground is sinking sand."

Christ is our solid rock. He does not change. He does not move. We move, we change, we allow the things of this world to penetrate us, to shift us, and before long...we have slipped from underneath his wing.

Can he snatch us up? YES! Can he bring us back? YES! But we have free will, and he wants us to WANT to be near him, to CHOOSE HIS WAY, to know we NEED to be near him. He will pursue us, no doubt, but the longer we resist, the longer we stay away, the bigger our consequences may be.

Where does one turn when one is lost, when one feels the pressure of this world? The first thing is you have to understand that faith is not circumstantial. Faith is based on a person, Jesus Christ. If we based our faith on circumstance, just imagine how wavering that would be. We rest our faith on Jesus, on our heavenly father, that he is who he said he is. "I am who I am."

"So now, since we have been made right in God's sight *by faith in his promises*, we can have real peace with Him because of what Jesus Christ our Lord has done for us" (Romans 5:1).

"Faith is hope taken one step further." God can do all things. Doesn't mean that he *will*, but he is still God. Your eternity is still secure even if your prayers are not answered. That's a PROMISE!

Things God did not promise: He did not promise you would not feel pain; he did not promise that you would not get sick; he did not promise you would be rich; he did not promise your kids would be fine and dandy; he did not promise you would get married; he did not promise that you would not lose someone that you love...Do I need to go on?

What he did promise is that he would never leave you; he did promise that if you come to him with an open heart, he would give you MERCY and GRACE every single time. *EVERY SINGLE TIME.*

He promised that he would love you all the days of your life, and when the road was too narrow, he would carry you if you let him.

> But we have this treasure in jars of clay to show that this all-surpassing power is from God and not from us. We are hard pressed on every side *but not crushed*; perplexed *but not abandoned*; struck down *but not destroyed.* We always carry around in our body the death of Jesus so that the life of Jesus may be revealed in our body. (2 Corinthians 4:7–10)

> "The path to heaven runs through suffering. Through the sorrow of the world, through that certain fog of doubt and pain, we have faith, sure of what we hope for, certain of what we do not see. God is love. God is in control. God will wipe away every tear and replace it with a river of joy."

These are words to soak up, words to hold on to in times of trouble. Things of this world will fail you, and they will not withstand the test of time. Satan is a liar; don't you know that by now? Tempting, slick, and always lurking. But Satan has NO POWER over God and no power over the spirit that lives in every single believer. Do not be fooled.

It's a journey...and it's not easy. Sometimes you are climbing up that hill and you think you are never going to make it. I think that way sometimes. I will get to a spot and feel as though I can't get my foot in the right spot to move forward. I want to...I need to...but I am weak. That is when you have to call on God and ask him for the Grace. Remember, God promised us Grace—"Grace is energy to endure. Grace is God's enduring power, his strength." Grace will get your foot in the right spot so you can pull yourself to the next level.

Look back on your life. Was there ever a time when God brought you all the way up to the top of the mountain...and then dropped you?

In troubled times do not look ahead; look behind, and you will see a life time of promises. You will see he has never forsaken you. He has always brought you through.

Assurance

A new year has arrived! The old one is gone, and everything in that year is behind us. Was it a good year for you? Did you accomplish much in your resolutions? Are you glad it's over, or was it such a great year you don't want to see it leave?

No matter what your answer is to those questions, you can be assured that God knew exactly what he was doing. What happened was exactly what he allowed to happen, and he wants you to be assured and confident that "all good will come for those that believe."

As we move into 2011, I was thinking, "What do I need the most? What would really be the best thing I could ask for, hope for, and want based on my own past year and what is ahead?" The word that comes to my mind is *assurance*.

I want to be assured that, no matter what comes my way this year, I will not be alone, that I will have strength to endure, that I will never lose hope, and that I can be thankful in all things. Wouldn't that be awesome if you had that? Assurance of those things would really cover any New Year's resolution I could have, right?

So I turn to the living word of God, the promises he made, and I find exactly what I need:

I am never alone: "Be strong and courageous. Do not be afraid or terrified because of them, for the Lord your God goes with you; he will never leave you nor forsake you" (Deuteronomy 31:6).

I will have strength to endure: "I can do all things in Christ who strengthens me" (Philippians 4:13).

I have assurance: "Now faith is confidence in what we hope for and assurance about what we do not see" (Hebrews 11:1).

I have hope: "Let us hold unswervingly to the hope we profess, for he who promised is faithful" (Hebrews 10:23).

I can be thankful: "And we know that in all things God works for the good for those who love him, who have been called according to his purpose" (Romans 8:28).

Forgiveness

This word has been all around me this past month. It's been in my devotionals, people I come into contact with have discussed it with me, and even the sermons at my church these last weeks bring this word to my mind and my spirit.

For some of us, forgiveness is such a difficult task. Sometimes we even think that we have forgiven someone their debt, yet when we talk about that person, not so pleasant things come out of our mouths. For some of us that are believers of Christ, we like to say, "God is working that area of my life," but the truth is God does not *work* that area. That is just our flesh wanting to stay in the unforgiveness. When you need forgiveness, does God need time to work that area, or does he give you grace right on the spot?

Matthew 5:24 reads, "Leave your gift there in front of the altar. First go and be reconciled to them; then come and offer your gift." It is so important to God that we reconcile with others that he does not want even to accept our gifts at the altar if we harbor ill feelings with anyone.

The Bible is so clear about forgiveness and reconciliation. When Jesus died on the cross, he said, "Father, forgive them for they do not know."

Now let's get a mental picture of this. Jesus, the sinless son of God, is hanging on a cross. Nail in each hand and his feet. He has been beaten, flogged, tortured…must have been in pain like no human could imagine. And the last thing he said was, "Father, forgive them." Do we show that kind of grace to others? Better yet, don't we want that kind of grace when we ask the Lord for forgiveness?

I know this is not an easy task. I have been abandoned by my parents, the ones who were supposed to love and protect me. I have been made fun of, taken advantage of, lied to, cheated on, betrayed, rejected, and the list goes on. So I *know* how hard it is to forgive someone who has done you wrong, hurt you so badly, or even hurt the ones you love the most…like your children. I did not wake up one day and all was forgiven. But when I realized how much *I* needed forgiveness, when I realized how much grace *I* receive every single time I ask for it, I had to take the steps to forgive, to reconcile. I would even fake it. I would say, "Lord, I know you want me to forgive this person, and I really want to forgive them, but I am mad and I am hurt. Help me to forgive them."

Here is a place to begin. Three things you can do:

- Who hurt you, and how? Write it out, see it on paper, and feel it as you remember it.
- Then tell yourself every day, "God loves [that person] too." Every time that person comes to your mind in a negative way, you must tell yourself that God loves him or her too.
- Never forget how you are forgiven by your heavenly father, with grace and a clean slate, every time you ask with a pure heart.

When you do something wrong, haven't you called upon the Lord and said, "Lord, have mercy on me," or "Lord, please forgive me"? How would you like the Lord to respond? Would you like him to respond the way that you do, or the way that HE does? Meaning this: you have done something that you know is not right, and you come to the Lord and say, "Lord, please have mercy on me, I'm sorry." Would you want the Lord to turn to you and say, "At this time I just can't forgive you," or "I need time to work through what you have done...I forgive you, but I can't forget about what you did"?

That looks sad even reading it, doesn't it? Here is why forgiveness is so important: God loves you so much he wants you to live an abundant life. He wants you to experience great joy and happiness. When you harbor ill feelings, you cannot enjoy life to the fullest, regardless of what you think. You may think that you live a perfectly wonderful life and that forgiving someone wouldn't change a thing. I disagree. Forgiveness frees *you*. It's the kind of freedom no money can buy and no one can give to you. It's a gift you receive once you forgive someone. And you also give them a gift: grace. "In him we have redemption through his blood, the forgiveness of sins, in accordance with the riches of God's grace" (Ephesians 1:7).

Forgiveness and love kind of go hand in hand. My February message was on love, and as I was writing I thought, "You know, to forgive someone who has done you wrong really is showing them Christ-like love. It's giving to that person when they deserve it the least but need it the most." That is what I said about love in February's message. We are called to love one another as Christ loved us. Forgive as you have been forgiven, and give grace as you would want grace given to you.

The Silver lining

"Every cloud has a silver lining." Have you ever said that? Have you ever felt that your "cloud" had a silver lining? I looked up what the definition of that would be, and here is what it said: "A hopeful or comforting prospect in the midst of difficulty."

When I read that, I thought, "Gee, that sounds like a Christian thing." After all, isn't Jesus a hopeful comfort in the midst of difficulty?

I started thinking about this whole thing while driving to work. I heard on the radio someone talking about Habitat for Humanity and how many houses have been built and families blessed by this organization. A family was without a home (dark cloud), and then their silver lining (hopeful/comforting prospect in the midst of difficulty) is that they are now blessed with one.

Truth is, we will all be in the dark cloud of something sometime in our life, and we can be quite certain it will be more than once. I believe the "silver lining" is the blessing in the midst of it. Do you look for the blessing in the midst of your difficult time? I know it is hard to do that, but when you do, you can have comfort and hope. If you are a believer in Christ, not only do you see the blessing, you have a constant companion during those times.

For me, 2010 was a really tough year. There was a "dark cloud" for most of it. I lost my home in February. In March my dad took ill out of the clear blue sky, and then in April he passed away. In May I found out I had cancer and had to have surgery, chemo, and then radiation. It was very hard for me to imagine there could be a "silver lining." I wanted to be "hopeful and look for the comforting prospect in the midst of the difficulty," but it was hard. I found myself many times laid out on the floor asking God to breathe on me. That is what I do when the day is too much for me, when I have more than I can handle. Funny, many people say, "God never puts on you more than you can handle," but I am here to tell you...oh yes he does. If he never put more on you than you can handle, you would have no need for him, right? You would rely on your own means; you would be self-sufficient instead of God sufficient.

What I can testify to is this: there is *always* a "silver lining," always "a hopeful or comforting prospect in the midst of difficulty." There is always comfort if you reach out and call upon your heavenly father. That does not mean you won't have to go through it. This I learned. But I had hope, I had comfort, and I had a constant companion who preceded my steps. "The Lord himself goes before you and will be with you; he will never leave you nor forsake you. Do not be afraid; do not be discouraged" (Deuteronomy 31:8).

Made in the USA
Charleston, SC
16 May 2015